# I AM *serious* ABOUT MY PLANNER

## IF YOU FIND IT, PLEASE CONTACT ME @

_____

NAME

_____

PHONE

_____

EMAIL ADDRESS

Pray Until Something Happens

Trust

Hope Faith

LOVE

Believe

# 2022
## *two thousand twenty-two*

### January 2022
| S | M | T | W | T | F | S |
|---|---|---|---|---|---|---|
|   |   |   |   |   |   | 1 |
| 2 | 3 | 4 | 5 | 6 | 7 | 8 |
| 9 | 10 | 11 | 12 | 13 | 14 | 15 |
| 16 | 17 | 18 | 19 | 20 | 21 | 22 |
| 23 | 24 | 25 | 26 | 27 | 28 | 29 |
| 30 | 31 |   |   |   |   |   |

### February 2022
| S | M | T | W | T | F | S |
|---|---|---|---|---|---|---|
|   |   | 1 | 2 | 3 | 4 | 5 |
| 6 | 7 | 8 | 9 | 10 | 11 | 12 |
| 13 | 14 | 15 | 16 | 17 | 18 | 19 |
| 20 | 21 | 22 | 23 | 24 | 25 | 26 |
| 27 | 28 |   |   |   |   |   |

### March 2022
| S | M | T | W | T | F | S |
|---|---|---|---|---|---|---|
|   |   | 1 | 2 | 3 | 4 | 5 |
| 6 | 7 | 8 | 9 | 10 | 11 | 12 |
| 13 | 14 | 15 | 16 | 17 | 18 | 19 |
| 20 | 21 | 22 | 23 | 24 | 25 | 26 |
| 27 | 28 | 29 | 30 | 31 |   |   |

### April 2022
| S | M | T | W | T | F | S |
|---|---|---|---|---|---|---|
|   |   |   |   |   | 1 | 2 |
| 3 | 4 | 5 | 6 | 7 | 8 | 9 |
| 10 | 11 | 12 | 13 | 14 | 15 | 16 |
| 17 | 18 | 19 | 20 | 21 | 22 | 23 |
| 24 | 25 | 26 | 27 | 28 | 29 | 30 |

### May 2022
| S | M | T | W | T | F | S |
|---|---|---|---|---|---|---|
| 1 | 2 | 3 | 4 | 5 | 6 | 7 |
| 8 | 9 | 10 | 11 | 12 | 13 | 14 |
| 15 | 16 | 17 | 18 | 19 | 20 | 21 |
| 22 | 23 | 24 | 25 | 26 | 27 | 28 |
| 29 | 30 | 31 |   |   |   |   |

### June 2022
| S | M | T | W | T | F | S |
|---|---|---|---|---|---|---|
|   |   |   | 1 | 2 | 3 | 4 |
| 5 | 6 | 7 | 8 | 9 | 10 | 11 |
| 12 | 13 | 14 | 15 | 16 | 17 | 18 |
| 19 | 20 | 21 | 22 | 23 | 24 | 25 |
| 26 | 27 | 28 | 29 | 30 |   |   |

### July 2022
| S | M | T | W | T | F | S |
|---|---|---|---|---|---|---|
|   |   |   |   |   | 1 | 2 |
| 3 | 4 | 5 | 6 | 7 | 8 | 9 |
| 10 | 11 | 12 | 13 | 14 | 15 | 16 |
| 17 | 18 | 19 | 20 | 21 | 22 | 23 |
| 24 | 25 | 26 | 27 | 28 | 29 | 30 |
| 31 |   |   |   |   |   |   |

### August 2022
| S | M | T | W | T | F | S |
|---|---|---|---|---|---|---|
|   | 1 | 2 | 3 | 4 | 5 | 6 |
| 7 | 8 | 9 | 10 | 11 | 12 | 13 |
| 14 | 15 | 16 | 17 | 18 | 19 | 20 |
| 21 | 22 | 23 | 24 | 25 | 26 | 27 |
| 28 | 29 | 30 | 31 |   |   |   |

### September 2022
| S | M | T | W | T | F | S |
|---|---|---|---|---|---|---|
|   |   |   |   | 1 | 2 | 3 |
| 4 | 5 | 6 | 7 | 8 | 9 | 10 |
| 11 | 12 | 13 | 14 | 15 | 16 | 17 |
| 18 | 19 | 20 | 21 | 22 | 23 | 24 |
| 25 | 26 | 27 | 28 | 29 | 30 |   |

### October 2022
| S | M | T | W | T | F | S |
|---|---|---|---|---|---|---|
|   |   |   |   |   |   | 1 |
| 2 | 3 | 4 | 5 | 6 | 7 | 8 |
| 9 | 10 | 11 | 12 | 13 | 14 | 15 |
| 16 | 17 | 18 | 19 | 20 | 21 | 22 |
| 23 | 24 | 25 | 26 | 27 | 28 | 29 |
| 30 | 31 |   |   |   |   |   |

### November 2022
| S | M | T | W | T | F | S |
|---|---|---|---|---|---|---|
|   |   | 1 | 2 | 3 | 4 | 5 |
| 6 | 7 | 8 | 9 | 10 | 11 | 12 |
| 13 | 14 | 15 | 16 | 17 | 18 | 19 |
| 20 | 21 | 22 | 23 | 24 | 25 | 26 |
| 27 | 28 | 29 | 30 |   |   |   |

### December 2022
| S | M | T | W | T | F | S |
|---|---|---|---|---|---|---|
|   |   |   |   | 1 | 2 | 3 |
| 4 | 5 | 6 | 7 | 8 | 9 | 10 |
| 11 | 12 | 13 | 14 | 15 | 16 | 17 |
| 18 | 19 | 20 | 21 | 22 | 23 | 24 |
| 25 | 26 | 27 | 28 | 29 | 30 | 31 |

## *Important Dates to Remember*

| | | | |
|---|---|---|---|
| New Year's Day | Sat 1/1 | Father's Day | Sun 6/19 |
| Martin L. King Jr. Day | Mon 1/17 | Independence Day | Mon 7/4 |
| Valentine's Day | Mon 2/14 | Labor Day | Mon 9/5 |
| Presidents' Day | Mon 2/21 | Columbus Day | Mon 10/10 |
| Daylight Savings Begins | Sun 3/13 | Halloween | Mon 10/31 |
| St. Patrick's Day | Thu 3/17 | Daylight Savings Ends | Sun 11/6 |
| Easter | Sun 4/17 | Veterans Day | Fri 11/11 |
| Earth Day | Fri 4/22 | Thanksgiving | Thu 11/24 |
| Mother's Day | Sun 5/8 | Christmas | Sun 12/25 |
| Memorial Day | Mon 5/30 | Kwanzaa Begins | Mon 12/26 |
| Juneteenth | Sun 6/19 | New Year's Eve | Sat 12/31 |

# Love Letter

Use the space below to write yourself a love letter.

_____

_____

_____

_____

_____

_____

_____

_____

_____

_____

*"I welcome positive change into every area of my life."*

| Sunday | Monday | Tuesday | Wednesday |
|--------|--------|---------|-----------|
|        |        |         |           |
| 3      | 4      | 5       | 6         |
| 10     | 11 Columbus Day | 12 | 13 |
| 17     | 18     | 19      | 20        |
| 24 / 31 Halloween | 25 | 26 | 27 |

| Thursday | Friday | Saturday |
|---|---|---|
| | 1 | 2 |
| 7 | 8 | 9 |
| 14 | 15 | 16 |
| 21 | 22 | 23 |
| 28 | 29 | 30 |

October 2021

| Sunday | Monday | Tuesday | Wednesday |
|---|---|---|---|
|  | 1 | 2<br><br>Election Day | 3 |
| 7<br><br>Daylight Savings Ends | 8 | 9 | 10 |
| 14 | 15 | 16 | 17 |
| 21 | 22 | 23 | 24 |
| 28 | 29 | 30 |  |

| Thursday | Friday | Saturday |
|---|---|---|
| 4 | 5 | 6 |
| 11<br><br>Veterans Day | 12 | 13 |
| 18 | 19 | 20 |
| 25<br><br>Thanksgiving | 26 | 27 |
|  |  |  |

November
2021

| Sunday | Monday | Tuesday | Wednesday |
|---|---|---|---|
|  |  |  | 1 |
| 5 | 6 | 7 | 8 |
| 12 | 13 | 14 | 15 |
| 19 | 20 | 21 | 22 |
| 26 Kwanzaa Begins | 27 | 28 | 29 |

| Thursday | Friday | Saturday |
|---|---|---|
| 2 | 3 | 4 |
| 9 | 10 | 11 |
| 16 | 17 | 18 |
| 23 | 24<br><br>Christmas Eve | 25<br><br>Christmas Day |
| 30 | 31<br><br>New Year's Eve | |

December 2021

# Create-A-Vision

"Write the vision; make it plain." -Habakkuk 2:2

**Don't forget!**
Come back to reflect on which visions came true.

Cut & paste, write or draw pictures and words that symbolize your vision for the first quarter of the year.

# Stuff I Need to Remember

_____

_____

_____

_____

_____

_____

_____

_____

_____

_____

Where you are a year from now
is a reflection of the choices
you choose to make now.

| Sunday | Monday | Tuesday | Wednesday |
|--------|--------|---------|-----------|
|        |        |         |           |
| 2      | 3      | 4       | 5         |
| 9      | 10     | 11      | 12        |
| 16     | 17     | 18      | 19        |
| 23 / 30 | 24 / 31 Dr. Martin Luther King Jr. Holiday | 25 | 26 |

| Thursday | Friday | Saturday |
|---|---|---|
| | | **1**<br><br>New Year's Day |
| **6** | **7** | **8** |
| **13** | **14** | **15** |
| **20** | **21** | **22** |
| **27** | **28** | **29** |

January

2022

I will walk by faith even when I cannot see. -2 Corinthians 5:7

Sunday 26

Monday 27

Tuesday 28

Wednesday 29

# December 2021 / January 2022

**Thursday** 30

**Friday** 31

New Year's Eve

**Saturday** 1

New Year's Day

## January

| S | M | T | W | T | F | S |
|---|---|---|---|---|---|---|
|   |   |   |   |   |   | 1 |
| 2 | 3 | 4 | 5 | 6 | 7 | 8 |
| 9 | 10 | 11 | 12 | 13 | 14 | 15 |
| 16 | 17 | 18 | 19 | 20 | 21 | 22 |
| 23 | 24 | 25 | 26 | 27 | 28 | 29 |
| 30 | 31 |   |   |   |   |   |

2022

I will walk by faith even when I cannot see. -2 Corinthians 5:7

Sunday 2

Monday 3

Tuesday 4

Wednesday 5

## Thursday 6

## Friday 7

## Saturday 8

## January

| S | M | T | W | T | F | S |
|---|---|---|---|---|---|---|
|   |   |   |   |   |   | 1 |
| 2 | 3 | 4 | 5 | 6 | 7 | 8 |
| 9 | 10 | 11 | 12 | 13 | 14 | 15 |
| 16 | 17 | 18 | 19 | 20 | 21 | 22 |
| 23 | 24 | 25 | 26 | 27 | 28 | 29 |
| 30 | 31 |   |   |   |   |   |

### 2022

I will walk by faith even when I cannot see. -2 Corinthians 5:7

Sunday 9

Monday 10

Tuesday 11

Wednesday 12

## Thursday 13

## Friday 14

## Saturday 15

### January

| S | M | T | W | T | F | S |
|---|---|---|---|---|---|---|
| | | | | | | 1 |
| 2 | 3 | 4 | 5 | 6 | 7 | 8 |
| 9 | 10 | 11 | 12 | 13 | 14 | 15 |
| 16 | 17 | 18 | 19 | 20 | 21 | 22 |
| 23 | 24 | 25 | 26 | 27 | 28 | 29 |
| 30 | 31 | | | | | |

**2022**

I will walk by faith even when I cannot see. -2 Corinthians 5:7

## Sunday 16

## Monday 17

Dr. Martin Luther King Jr. Day

## Tuesday 18

## Wednesday 19

## Thursday 20

## Friday 21

## Saturday 22

### January

| S | M | T | W | T | F | S |
|---|---|---|---|---|---|---|
|   |   |   |   |   |   | 1 |
| 2 | 3 | 4 | 5 | 6 | 7 | 8 |
| 9 | 10 | 11 | 12 | 13 | 14 | 15 |
| 16 | 17 | 18 | 19 | 20 | 21 | 22 |
| 23 | 24 | 25 | 26 | 27 | 28 | 29 |
| 30 | 31 |   |   |   |   |   |

**2022**

Sunday 23

Monday 24

Tuesday 25

Wednesday 26

Thursday 27

Friday 28

Saturday 29

# January

| S | M | T | W | T | F | S |
|---|---|---|---|---|---|---|
|   |   |   |   |   |   | 1 |
| 2 | 3 | 4 | 5 | 6 | 7 | 8 |
| 9 | 10 | 11 | 12 | 13 | 14 | 15 |
| 16 | 17 | 18 | 19 | 20 | 21 | 22 |
| 23 | 24 | 25 | 26 | 27 | 28 | 29 |
| 30 | 31 |   |   |   |   |   |

2022

Become so
confident in who
you are that no ones
opinion, rejection or
behavior can rock you.

Color Me

# WHERE FOCUS GOES
*energy flows*

## goal:

## STEP 1:

## STEP 2:

## STEP 3:

A *goal* WITHOUT A *plan* IS A *wish*

# Gratitude List

♡

♡

♡

♡

♡

## CONSISTENCY WILL TRANSFORM
*average into excellence*

# Stuff I Need to Remember

_____

_____

_____

_____

_____

_____

_____

_____

_____

Just breathe ~ Have faith that everything
will work out for the BEST.

| Sunday | Monday | Tuesday | Wednesday |
|---|---|---|---|
| | | 1 | 2 |
| 6 | 7 | 8 | 9 |
| 13 | 14<br><br>Valentine's Day | 15 | 16 |
| 20 | 21<br><br>President's Day | 22 | 23 |
| 27 | 28 | | |

| Thursday | Friday | Saturday |
|---|---|---|
| 3 | 4 | 5 |
| 10 | 11 | 12 |
| 17 | 18 | 19 |
| 24 | 25 | 26 |
| | | |

February

2022

Sunday 30

Monday 31

Tuesday 1

Wednesday 2

Thursday 3

Friday 4

Saturday 5

## February

| S | M | T | W | T | F | S |
|---|---|---|---|---|---|---|
|  |  | 1 | 2 | 3 | 4 | 5 |
| 6 | 7 | 8 | 9 | 10 | 11 | 12 |
| 13 | 14 | 15 | 16 | 17 | 18 | 19 |
| 20 | 21 | 22 | 23 | 24 | 25 | 26 |
| 27 | 28 |  |  |  |  |  |

2022

Sunday 6

Monday 7

Tuesday 8

Wednesday 9

## Thursday 10

## Friday 11

## Saturday 12

### February

| S | M | T | W | T | F | S |
|---|---|---|---|---|---|---|
| | | 1 | 2 | 3 | 4 | 5 |
| 6 | 7 | 8 | 9 | 10 | 11 | 12 |
| 13 | 14 | 15 | 16 | 17 | 18 | 19 |
| 20 | 21 | 22 | 23 | 24 | 25 | 26 |
| 27 | 28 | | | | | |

2022

Sunday **13**

Monday **14**

Valentine's Day

Tuesday **15**

Wednesday **16**

## Thursday 17

## Friday 18

## Saturday 19

### February

| S | M | T | W | T | F | S |
|---|---|---|---|---|---|---|
|   |   | 1 | 2 | 3 | 4 | 5 |
| 6 | 7 | 8 | 9 | 10 | 11 | 12 |
| 13 | 14 | 15 | 16 | 17 | 18 | 19 |
| 20 | 21 | 22 | 23 | 24 | 25 | 26 |
| 27 | 28 |   |   |   |   |   |

### 2022

# You are an overcomer. -Romans 8:37

## Sunday 20

## Monday 21

Presidents' Day

## Tuesday 22

## Wednesday 23

## Thursday 24

## Friday 25

## Saturday 26

### February

| S | M | T | W | T | F | S |
|---|---|---|---|---|---|---|
|   |   | 1 | 2 | 3 | 4 | 5 |
| 6 | 7 | 8 | 9 | 10 | 11 | 12 |
| 13 | 14 | 15 | 16 | 17 | 18 | 19 |
| 20 | 21 | 22 | 23 | 24 | 25 | 26 |
| 27 | 28 |   |   |   |   |   |

2022

# Inflammation Relief Tea

*Recipe provided by contest winner: Mary Harris, Washington D.C.*

## INGREDIENTS:
2 pineapples
1 ginger root
1 turmeric root
1 lemon

## PREP WORK:
~Cut up pineapple into chunks.
~Chop up both the ginger and
tumeric roots into thick slices.
~Cut up lemon into slices.

## INSTRUCTIONS:
~Bring pot of water to a boil.
~Add ingredients to water and
let boil for 30 minutes.
~Remove from fire and let the
mixtue sit for 5 minutes.
~Pour through a strainer
into a pitcher.
~Serve hot or iced.

# FIND THE WORDS BELOW IN THE SEARCH:

GBABY    GENUINE    GRATITUDE    GENTLE    GRACE
GOODNESS    GLORY    GOD    GUIDANCE    GENIUS

```
Q  G  G  E  N  U  I  N  E  G
H  B  G  L  O  Q  X  T  C  U
U  G  O  O  D  N  E  S  S  I
G  P  U  L  R  D  S  G  A  D
B  R  D  I  U  H  C  R  R  L
B  V  A  E  D  S  T  A  G  Z
A  M  G  T  G  A  J  C  S  G
Y  A  G  E  I  W  N  E  U  L
U  I  E  Y  I  T  G  C  I  O
G  E  N  I  U  S  U  G  E  R
O  N  T  U  D  E  G  D  T  Y
O  E  L  G  B  A  B  Y  E  L
D  G  E  O  G  O  D  R  A  P
```

# WHERE FOCUS GOES
*energy flows*

## goal:

## STEP 1:

## STEP 2:

## STEP 3:

A *goal* WITHOUT A *plan* IS A *wish*

# Gratitude List

♡

♡

♡

♡

♡

**SELF LOVE** *isn't selfish*

# Stuff I Need to Remember

_____

_____

_____

_____

_____

_____

_____

_____

_____

NEVER apologize for having high standards. People who really want to be in your life will rise up to meet them.

Soul Garden

| Sunday | Monday | Tuesday | Wednesday |
|--------|--------|---------|-----------|
|        |        | 1       | 2         |
| 6      | 7      | 8       | 9         |
| 13 <br> Daylight Savings | 14 | 15 | 16 |
| 20     | 21     | 22      | 23        |
| 27     | 28     | 29      | 30        |

| Thursday | Friday | Saturday |
|---|---|---|
| 3 | 4 | 5 |
| 10 | 11 | 12 |
| 17<br><br>St. Patrick's Day | 18 | 19 |
| 24 | 25 | 26 |
| 31 | | |

March

2022

## Sunday 27

## Monday 28

## Tuesday 1

## Wednesday 2

## Thursday 3

## Friday 4

## Saturday 5

### March

| S | M | T | W | T | F | S |
|---|---|---|---|---|---|---|
|   |   | 1 | 2 | 3 | 4 | 5 |
| 6 | 7 | 8 | 9 | 10 | 11 | 12 |
| 13 | 14 | 15 | 16 | 17 | 18 | 19 |
| 20 | 21 | 22 | 23 | 24 | 25 | 26 |
| 27 | 28 | 29 | 30 | 31 |   |   |

2022

## Sunday 6

## Monday 7

## Tuesday 8

## Wednesday 9

## Thursday 10

## Friday 11

## Saturday 12

### March

| S | M | T | W | T | F | S |
|---|---|---|---|---|---|---|
|   |   | 1 | 2 | 3 | 4 | 5 |
| 6 | 7 | 8 | 9 | 10 | 11 | 12 |
| 13 | 14 | 15 | 16 | 17 | 18 | 19 |
| 20 | 21 | 22 | 23 | 24 | 25 | 26 |
| 27 | 28 | 29 | 30 | 31 |   |   |

2022

Sunday                    *13*

Daylight Savings Begins

Monday                    *14*

Tuesday                   *15*

Wednesday                 *16*

## Thursday 17

St. Patrick's Day

## Friday 18

## Saturday 19

### March

| S | M | T | W | T | F | S |
|---|---|---|---|---|---|---|
|  |  | 1 | 2 | 3 | 4 | 5 |
| 6 | 7 | 8 | 9 | 10 | 11 | 12 |
| 13 | 14 | 15 | 16 | 17 | 18 | 19 |
| 20 | 21 | 22 | 23 | 24 | 25 | 26 |
| 27 | 28 | 29 | 30 | 31 |  |  |

2022

Who can find a worthy woman for her price is above rubies. -Proverbs 31:10

Sunday 20

Monday 21

Tuesday 22

Wednesday 23

Thursday 24

Friday 25

Saturday 26

## March

| S | M | T | W | T | F | S |
|---|---|---|---|---|---|---|
|   |   | 1 | 2 | 3 | 4 | 5 |
| 6 | 7 | 8 | 9 | 10 | 11 | 12 |
| 13 | 14 | 15 | 16 | 17 | 18 | 19 |
| 20 | 21 | 22 | 23 | 24 | 25 | 26 |
| 27 | 28 | 29 | 30 | 31 |   |   |

2022

# Create-A-Vision

"Write the vision; make it plain." -Habakkuk 2:2

**Don't forget!**
Come back to reflect on which visions came true.

Cut & paste, write or draw pictures and words that symbolize your vision for the first quarter of the year.

# WHERE FOCUS GOES
*energy flows*

**goal:**

## STEP 1:

## STEP 2:

## STEP 3:

A *goal* WITHOUT A *plan* IS A *wish*

# Gratitude List

♡

♡

♡

♡

♡

## BE OBSESSED
*with your own potential*

# Stuff I Need to Remember

_____

_____

_____

_____

_____

_____

_____

_____

_____

Don't stop shining just because
someone is intimidated by your light.

| Sunday | Monday | Tuesday | Wednesday |
|---|---|---|---|
| | | | |
| 3 | 4 | 5 | 6 |
| 10 | 11 | 12 | 13 |
| 17 | 18 | 19 | 20 |
| Easter | | | |
| 24 | 25 | 26 | 27 |

| Thursday | Friday | Saturday |
|---|---|---|
| | 1 | 2 |
| 7 | 8 | 9 |
| 14 | 15 | 16 |
| 21 | 22 | 23 |
| 28 | Earth Day<br>29 | 30 |

April

2022

# I can do all things through Christ. -Phillippians 4:13

Sunday 27

Monday 28

Tuesday 29

Wednesday 30

Thursday 31

Friday 1

Saturday 2

## April

| S | M | T | W | T | F | S |
|---|---|---|---|---|---|---|
|   |   |   |   |   | 1 | 2 |
| 3 | 4 | 5 | 6 | 7 | 8 | 9 |
| 10 | 11 | 12 | 13 | 14 | 15 | 16 |
| 17 | 18 | 19 | 20 | 21 | 22 | 23 |
| 24 | 25 | 26 | 27 | 28 | 29 | 30 |

2022

| Sunday 3 | Monday 4 |
|---|---|
| Tuesday 5 | Wednesday 6 |

## Thursday 7

## Friday 8

## Saturday 9

### April

| S | M | T | W | T | F | S |
|---|---|---|---|---|---|---|
| | | | | | 1 | 2 |
| 3 | 4 | 5 | 6 | 7 | 8 | 9 |
| 10 | 11 | 12 | 13 | 14 | 15 | 16 |
| 17 | 18 | 19 | 20 | 21 | 22 | 23 |
| 24 | 25 | 26 | 27 | 28 | 29 | 30 |

2022

# I can do all things through Christ. -Phillippians 4:13

## Sunday
10

## Monday
11

## Tuesday
12

## Wednesday
13

## Thursday 14

## Friday 15

## Saturday 16

### April

| S | M | T | W | T | F | S |
|---|---|---|---|---|---|---|
| | | | | | 1 | 2 |
| 3 | 4 | 5 | 6 | 7 | 8 | 9 |
| 10 | 11 | 12 | 13 | 14 | 15 | 16 |
| 17 | 18 | 19 | 20 | 21 | 22 | 23 |
| 24 | 25 | 26 | 27 | 28 | 29 | 30 |

### 2022

# I can do all things through Christ. -Phillippians 4:13

| Sunday | 17 | Monday | 18 |

Easter

| Tuesday | 19 | Wednesday | 20 |

## Thursday 21

## Friday 22

Earth Day

## Saturday 23

### April

| S | M | T | W | T | F | S |
|---|---|---|---|---|---|---|
| | | | | | 1 | 2 |
| 3 | 4 | 5 | 6 | 7 | 8 | 9 |
| 10 | 11 | 12 | 13 | 14 | 15 | 16 |
| 17 | 18 | 19 | 20 | 21 | 22 | 23 |
| 24 | 25 | 26 | 27 | 28 | 29 | 30 |

2022

Sunday 24

Monday 25

Tuesday 26

Wednesday 27

## Thursday 28

## Friday 29

## Saturday 30

### April

| S | M | T | W | T | F | S |
|---|---|---|---|---|---|---|
|  |  |  |  |  | 1 | 2 |
| 3 | 4 | 5 | 6 | 7 | 8 | 9 |
| 10 | 11 | 12 | 13 | 14 | 15 | 16 |
| 17 | 18 | 19 | 20 | 21 | 22 | 23 |
| 24 | 25 | 26 | 27 | 28 | 29 | 30 |

2022

# Watermelon Lemonade Slushies

**INGREDIENTS:**
4 cups of watermelon
2 cups of lemonade
1 handful of raspberries
ice* -if needed

**PREP WORK:**
~Cut up watermelon into cubes.
~Freeze the watermelon cubes.

**INSTRUCTIONS:**
~In a blender, add your frozen watermelon cubes.
~Pour in the 2 cups of lemonade.
~Add a handful of raspberries.
~Blend until slushie reaches your desired consistency.
~Optional: add more ice as needed.

Color Me

# WHERE FOCUS GOES
*energy flows*

## goal:

## STEP 1:

## STEP 2:

## STEP 3:

A
*goal*
**WITHOUT A**
*plan*
**IS A**
*wish*

# Gratitude List

♡

♡

♡

♡

♡

## CONFIDENCE
*has no competition*

# Stuff I Need to Remember

_____

_____

_____

_____

_____

_____

_____

_____

_____

_____

When you start seeing your worth,
you'll find it harder to stay around
people who don't.

| Sunday | Monday | Tuesday | Wednesday |
|--------|--------|---------|-----------|
| 1 | 2 | 3 | 4 |
| 8<br><br>Mother's Day | 9 | 10 | 11 |
| 15 | 16 | 17 | 18 |
| 22 | 23 | 24 | 25 |
| 29 | 30<br><br>Memorial Day | 31 | |

| Thursday | Friday | Saturday |
|---|---|---|
| 5 | 6 | 7 |
| 12 | 13 | 14 |
| 19 | 20 | 21 |
| 26 | 27 | 28 |
| | | |

May

2022

The Lord will stand with you and give you strength. -2 Timothy 4:17

Sunday *1*

Monday *2*

Tuesday *3*

Wednesday *4*

## Thursday 5

## Friday 6

## Saturday 7

## May

| S | M | T | W | T | F | S |
|---|---|---|---|---|---|---|
| 1 | 2 | 3 | 4 | 5 | 6 | 7 |
| 8 | 9 | 10 | 11 | 12 | 13 | 14 |
| 15 | 16 | 17 | 18 | 19 | 20 | 21 |
| 22 | 23 | 24 | 25 | 26 | 27 | 28 |
| 29 | 30 | 31 | | | | |

2022

## Sunday 8

Mother's Day

## Monday 9

## Tuesday 10

## Wednesday 11

## Thursday *12*

## Friday *13*

## Saturday *14*

### May

| S | M | T | W | T | F | S |
|---|---|---|---|---|---|---|
| 1 | 2 | 3 | 4 | 5 | 6 | 7 |
| 8 | 9 | 10 | 11 | 12 | 13 | 14 |
| 15 | 16 | 17 | 18 | 19 | 20 | 21 |
| 22 | 23 | 24 | 25 | 26 | 27 | 28 |
| 29 | 30 | 31 | | | | |

**2022**

The Lord will stand with you and give you strength. -2 Timothy 4:17

Sunday 15

Monday 16

Tuesday 17

Wednesday 18

## Thursday 19

## Friday 20

## Saturday 21

### May

| S | M | T | W | T | F | S |
|---|---|---|---|---|---|---|
| 1 | 2 | 3 | 4 | 5 | 6 | 7 |
| 8 | 9 | 10 | 11 | 12 | 13 | 14 |
| 15 | 16 | 17 | 18 | 19 | 20 | 21 |
| 22 | 23 | 24 | 25 | 26 | 27 | 28 |
| 29 | 30 | 31 | | | | |

2022

Sunday 22

Monday 23

Tuesday 24

Wednesday 25

## Thursday 26

## Friday 27

## Saturday 28

### May

| S | M | T | W | T | F | S |
|---|---|---|---|---|---|---|
| 1 | 2 | 3 | 4 | 5 | 6 | 7 |
| 8 | 9 | 10 | 11 | 12 | 13 | 14 |
| 15 | 16 | 17 | 18 | 19 | 20 | 21 |
| 22 | 23 | 24 | 25 | 26 | 27 | 28 |
| 29 | 30 | 31 | | | | |

2022

# WHERE FOCUS GOES
*energy flows*

*goal:*

## STEP 1:

## STEP 2:

## STEP 3:

A *goal* WITHOUT A *plan* IS A *wish*

# Gratitude List

♡

♡

♡

♡

## KINDNESS IS FREE
*sprinkle it everywhere*

# Stuff I Need to Remember

_____

_____

_____

_____

_____

_____

_____

_____

_____

_____

The secret to your future is hidden
in your daily routine.

| Sunday | Monday | Tuesday | Wednesday |
|---|---|---|---|
| | | | 1 |
| 5 | 6 | 7 | 8 |
| 12 | 13 | 14 | 15 |
| 19<br><br>Father's Day /<br>Juneteenth | 20 | 21 | 22 |
| 26 | 27 | 28 | 29 |

| Thursday | Friday | Saturday |
|---|---|---|
| 2 | 3 | 4 |
| 9 | 10 | 11 |
| 16 | 17 | 18 |
| 23 | 24 | 25 |
| 30 | | |

June
2022

Kind words are like honey, sweet to the soul. -Proverbs 16:24

| Sunday | 29 |
| Monday | 30 |

Memorial Day

| Tuesday | 31 |
| Wednesday | 1 |

Thursday *2*

Friday *3*

Saturday *4*

## June

| S | M | T | W | T | F | S |
|---|---|---|---|---|---|---|
|   |   |   | 1 | 2 | 3 | 4 |
| 5 | 6 | 7 | 8 | 9 | 10 | 11 |
| 12 | 13 | 14 | 15 | 16 | 17 | 18 |
| 19 | 20 | 21 | 22 | 23 | 24 | 25 |
| 26 | 27 | 28 | 29 | 30 |   |   |

*2022*

Sunday                                    5

Monday                                    6

Tuesday                                   7

Wednesday                                 8

## Thursday 9

## Friday 10

## Saturday 11

### June

| S | M | T | W | T | F | S |
|---|---|---|---|---|---|---|
|   |   |   | 1 | 2 | 3 | 4 |
| 5 | 6 | 7 | 8 | 9 | 10 | 11 |
| 12 | 13 | 14 | 15 | 16 | 17 | 18 |
| 19 | 20 | 21 | 22 | 23 | 24 | 25 |
| 26 | 27 | 28 | 29 | 30 |   |   |

### 2022

Kind words are like honey, sweet to the soul. -Proverbs 16:24

## Sunday 12

## Monday 13

## Tuesday 14

## Wednesday 15

## Thursday 16

## Friday 17

## Saturday 18

## June

| S | M | T | W | T | F | S |
|---|---|---|---|---|---|---|
|   |   |   | 1 | 2 | 3 | 4 |
| 5 | 6 | 7 | 8 | 9 | 10 | 11 |
| 12 | 13 | 14 | 15 | 16 | 17 | 18 |
| 19 | 20 | 21 | 22 | 23 | 24 | 25 |
| 26 | 27 | 28 | 29 | 30 |   |   |

## 2022

## Sunday 19

Father's Day / Juneteenth

## Monday 20

## Tuesday 21

## Wednesday 22

## Thursday 23

## Friday 24

## Saturday 25

### June

| S | M | T | W | T | F | S |
|---|---|---|---|---|---|---|
|   |   |   | 1 | 2 | 3 | 4 |
| 5 | 6 | 7 | 8 | 9 | 10 | 11 |
| 12 | 13 | 14 | 15 | 16 | 17 | 18 |
| 19 | 20 | 21 | 22 | 23 | 24 | 25 |
| 26 | 27 | 28 | 29 | 30 |   |   |

### 2022

# Create-A-Vision

"Write the vision; make it plain." -Habakkuk 2:2

Cut & paste, write or draw pictures and words that symbolize your vision for the first quarter of the year.

# WHERE FOCUS GOES
*energy flows*

**goal:**

**STEP 1:**

**STEP 2:**

**STEP 3:**

A *goal* WITHOUT A *plan* IS A *wish*

# Gratitude List

♡

♡

♡

♡

♡

## CELEBRATE
every win, Big and Small

# Stuff I Need to Remember

_____

_____

_____

_____

_____

_____

_____

_____

_____

_____

Always expect something wonderful
to happen everyday.

| Sunday | Monday | Tuesday | Wednesday |
|--------|--------|---------|-----------|
|        |        |         |           |
| 3      | 4      | 5       | 6         |
|        | Independence Day |  |        |
| 10     | 11     | 12      | 13        |
| 17     | 18     | 19      | 20        |
| 24 / 31 | 25    | 26      | 27        |

| Thursday | Friday | Saturday |
|---|---|---|
| | 1 | 2 |
| 7 | 8 | 9 |
| 14 | 15 | 16 |
| 21 | 22 | 23 |
| 28 | 29 | 30 |

July
2022

Sunday 26

Monday 27

Tuesday 28

Wednesday 29

**Thursday** 30

**Friday** 1

**Saturday** 2

## July

| S | M | T | W | T | F | S |
|---|---|---|---|---|---|---|
|   |   |   |   |   | 1 | 2 |
| 3 | 4 | 5 | 6 | 7 | 8 | 9 |
| 10 | 11 | 12 | 13 | 14 | 15 | 16 |
| 17 | 18 | 19 | 20 | 21 | 22 | 23 |
| 24 | 25 | 26 | 27 | 28 | 29 | 30 |
| 31 |   |   |   |   |   |   |

**2022**

# Faith is not knowing God can, it's knowing He will.

## Sunday
3

## Monday
4

Independence Day

## Tuesday
5

## Wednesday
6

## Thursday 7

## Friday 8

## Saturday 9

# July

| S | M | T | W | T | F | S |
|---|---|---|---|---|---|---|
|  |  |  |  |  | 1 | 2 |
| 3 | 4 | 5 | 6 | 7 | 8 | 9 |
| 10 | 11 | 12 | 13 | 14 | 15 | 16 |
| 17 | 18 | 19 | 20 | 21 | 22 | 23 |
| 24 | 25 | 26 | 27 | 28 | 29 | 30 |
| 31 |  |  |  |  |  |  |

## 2022

# Faith is not knowing God can, it's knowing He will.

## Sunday
10

## Monday
11

## Tuesday
12

## Wednesday
13

## Thursday 14

## Friday 15

## Saturday 16

### July

| S | M | T | W | T | F | S |
|---|---|---|---|---|---|---|
| | | | | | 1 | 2 |
| 3 | 4 | 5 | 6 | 7 | 8 | 9 |
| 10 | 11 | 12 | 13 | 14 | 15 | 16 |
| 17 | 18 | 19 | 20 | 21 | 22 | 23 |
| 24 | 25 | 26 | 27 | 28 | 29 | 30 |
| 31 | | | | | | |

2022

# Faith is not knowing God can, it's knowing He will.

## Sunday 17

## Monday 18

## Tuesday 19

## Wednesday 20

## Thursday 21

## Friday 22

## Saturday 23

# July

| S | M | T | W | T | F | S |
|---|---|---|---|---|---|---|
| | | | | | 1 | 2 |
| 3 | 4 | 5 | 6 | 7 | 8 | 9 |
| 10 | 11 | 12 | 13 | 14 | 15 | 16 |
| 17 | 18 | 19 | 20 | 21 | 22 | 23 |
| 24 | 25 | 26 | 27 | 28 | 29 | 30 |
| 31 | | | | | | |

2022

# Faith is not knowing God can, it's knowing He will.

## Sunday
24

## Monday
25

## Tuesday
26

## Wednesday
27

## Thursday 28

## Friday 29

## Saturday 30

### July

| S | M | T | W | T | F | S |
|---|---|---|---|---|---|---|
| | | | | | 1 | 2 |
| 3 | 4 | 5 | 6 | 7 | 8 | 9 |
| 10 | 11 | 12 | 13 | 14 | 15 | 16 |
| 17 | 18 | 19 | 20 | 21 | 22 | 23 |
| 24 | 25 | 26 | 27 | 28 | 29 | 30 |
| 31 | | | | | | |

### 2022

# Feel Good Smoothie
## *Immunity Booster*

**INGREDIENTS:**

1 large orange
1/2 medium banana
1 cup of frozen mango chunks
1/2 cup of almond milk
1/4 teaspoon of vanilla extract

**PREP WORK:**

~Peel and slice orange
~Peel and slice banana

**INSTRUCTIONS:**

~In a blender, add your frozen
mango chunks, orange
and banana slices
~Pour in the 1/2 cup of
almond milk
~Add 1/4 teaspoon of
vanilla extract
~Blend until smoothie reaches
your desired consistency

# WHERE FOCUS GOES
*energy flows*

**goal:**

## STEP 1:

## STEP 2:

## STEP 3:

A *goal* WITHOUT A *plan* IS A *wish*

# Gratitude List

♡

♡

♡

♡

♡

## BE THE ENERGY
*you wish to attract*

# Stuff I Need to Remember

_____

_____

_____

_____

_____

_____

_____

_____

_____

You were created to be
VICTORIOUS.

| Sunday | Monday | Tuesday | Wednesday |
|---|---|---|---|
|  | 1 | 2 | 3 |
| 7 | 8 | 9 | 10 |
| 14 | 15 | 16 | 17 |
| 21 | 22 | 23 | 24 |
| 28 | 29 | 30 | 31 |

| Thursday | Friday | Saturday |
|---|---|---|
| 4 | 5 | 6 |
| 11 | 12 | 13 |
| 18 | 19 | 20 |
| 25 | 26 | 27 |
| | | |

August
2022

Sunday                              31


Monday                               1


Tuesday                              2


Wednesday                            3

**Thursday** 4

**Friday** 5

**Saturday** 6

## August

| S | M | T | W | T | F | S |
|---|---|---|---|---|---|---|
|   | 1 | 2 | 3 | 4 | 5 | 6 |
| 7 | 8 | 9 | 10 | 11 | 12 | 13 |
| 14 | 15 | 16 | 17 | 18 | 19 | 20 |
| 21 | 22 | 23 | 24 | 25 | 26 | 27 |
| 28 | 29 | 30 | 31 |   |   |   |

**2022**

When the time is right, the Lord will make it happen. -Isaiah 60:22

## Sunday                                          7

## Monday                                          8

## Tuesday                                         9

## Wednesday                                      10

## Thursday 11

## Friday 12

## Saturday 13

### August

| S | M | T | W | T | F | S |
|---|---|---|---|---|---|---|
|   | 1 | 2 | 3 | 4 | 5 | 6 |
| 7 | 8 | 9 | 10 | 11 | 12 | 13 |
| 14 | 15 | 16 | 17 | 18 | 19 | 20 |
| 21 | 22 | 23 | 24 | 25 | 26 | 27 |
| 28 | 29 | 30 | 31 |   |   |   |

### 2022

Sunday 14

Monday 15

Tuesday 16

Wednesday 17

## Thursday 18

## Friday 19

## Saturday 20

### August

| S | M | T | W | T | F | S |
|---|---|---|---|---|---|---|
|   | 1 | 2 | 3 | 4 | 5 | 6 |
| 7 | 8 | 9 | 10 | 11 | 12 | 13 |
| 14 | 15 | 16 | 17 | 18 | 19 | 20 |
| 21 | 22 | 23 | 24 | 25 | 26 | 27 |
| 28 | 29 | 30 | 31 |   |   |   |

### 2022

Sunday *21*

Monday *22*

Tuesday *23*

Wednesday *24*

## Thursday 25

## Friday 26

## Saturday 27

# August

| S | M | T | W | T | F | S |
|---|---|---|---|---|---|---|
| | 1 | 2 | 3 | 4 | 5 | 6 |
| 7 | 8 | 9 | 10 | 11 | 12 | 13 |
| 14 | 15 | 16 | 17 | 18 | 19 | 20 |
| 21 | 22 | 23 | 24 | 25 | 26 | 27 |
| 28 | 29 | 30 | 31 | | | |

## 2022

# WHERE FOCUS GOES
## energy flows

**goal:**

**STEP 1:**

**STEP 2:**

**STEP 3:**

A *goal* WITHOUT A *plan* IS A *wish*

# Gratitude List

♡

♡

♡

♡

♡

## YOU ARE
*powerful, brilliant & brave*

# Stuff I Need to Remember

_____

_____

_____

_____

_____

_____

_____

_____

_____

If you want to find out how rich you are,
find out how many things you have
that money can't buy.

| Sunday | Monday | Tuesday | Wednesday |
|--------|--------|---------|-----------|
|        |        |         |           |
| 4      | 5      | 6       | 7         |
|        | Labor Day |      |           |
| 11     | 12     | 13      | 14        |
| 18     | 19     | 20      | 21        |
| 25     | 26     | 27      | 28        |

| Thursday | Friday | Saturday |
|---|---|---|
| 1 | 2 | 3 |
| 8 | 9 | 10 |
| 15 | 16 | 17 |
| 22 | 23 | 24 |
| 29 | 30 | |

September 2022

| Sunday | 28 | Monday | 29 |
|---|---|---|---|
|  |  |  |  |

| Tuesday | 30 | Wednesday | 31 |
|---|---|---|---|
|  |  |  |  |

## Thursday 1

## Friday 2

## Saturday 3

### September

| S | M | T | W | T | F | S |
|---|---|---|---|---|---|---|
|   |   |   |   | 1 | 2 | 3 |
| 4 | 5 | 6 | 7 | 8 | 9 | 10 |
| 11 | 12 | 13 | 14 | 15 | 16 | 17 |
| 18 | 19 | 20 | 21 | 22 | 23 | 24 |
| 25 | 26 | 27 | 28 | 29 | 30 |   |

2022

## The Lord is on my side; I will not fear. -Psalm 118:6

### Sunday
4

### Monday
5

Labor Day

### Tuesday
6

### Wednesday
7

## Thursday 8

## Friday 9

## Saturday 10

### September

| S | M | T | W | T | F | S |
|---|---|---|---|---|---|---|
|  |  |  |  | 1 | 2 | 3 |
| 4 | 5 | 6 | 7 | 8 | 9 | 10 |
| 11 | 12 | 13 | 14 | 15 | 16 | 17 |
| 18 | 19 | 20 | 21 | 22 | 23 | 24 |
| 25 | 26 | 27 | 28 | 29 | 30 |  |

2022

Sunday                    11

Monday                    12

Tuesday                   13

Wednesday                 14

## Thursday 15

## Friday 16

## Saturday 17

### September

| S | M | T | W | T | F | S |
|---|---|---|---|---|---|---|
| | | | | 1 | 2 | 3 |
| 4 | 5 | 6 | 7 | 8 | 9 | 10 |
| 11 | 12 | 13 | 14 | 15 | 16 | 17 |
| 18 | 19 | 20 | 21 | 22 | 23 | 24 |
| 25 | 26 | 27 | 28 | 29 | 30 | |

2022

Sunday 18

Monday 19

Tuesday 20

Wednesday 21

Thursday 22

Friday 23

Saturday 24

## September

| S | M | T | W | T | F | S |
|---|---|---|---|---|---|---|
|   |   |   |   | 1 | 2 | 3 |
| 4 | 5 | 6 | 7 | 8 | 9 | 10 |
| 11 | 12 | 13 | 14 | 15 | 16 | 17 |
| 18 | 19 | 20 | 21 | 22 | 23 | 24 |
| 25 | 26 | 27 | 28 | 29 | 30 |   |

2022

# Create-A-Vision

"Write the vision; make it plain." -Habakkuk 2:2

Cut & paste, write or draw pictures and words that symbolize your vision for the first quarter of the year.

# WHERE FOCUS GOES
*energy flows*

**goal:**

**STEP 1:**

**STEP 2:**

**STEP 3:**

A *goal* WITHOUT A *plan* IS A *wish*

# Gratitude List

♡

♡

♡

♡

♡

## GREAT THINGS NEVER
### came from comfort zones

# Stuff I Need to Remember

_____

_____

_____

_____

_____

_____

_____

_____

_____

Your body is your most pricelss possession
- take care of it.

Red Aura

Gbaby

| Sunday | Monday | Tuesday | Wednesday |
|--------|--------|---------|-----------|
|  |  |  |  |
| 2 | 3 | 4 | 5 |
| 9 | 10 Columbus Day | 11 | 12 |
| 16 | 17 | 18 | 19 |
| 23 / 30 | 24 / 31 Halloween | 25 | 26 |

| Thursday | Friday | Saturday |
|---|---|---|
| | | 1 |
| 6 | 7 | 8 |
| 13 | 14 | 15 |
| 20 | 21 | 22 |
| 27 | 28 | 29 |

October
2022

All things work together for those that love God. -Romans 8:28

Sunday                    25

Monday                    26

Tuesday                   27

Wednesday                 28

**Thursday** 29

**Friday** 30

**Saturday** 1

## October

| S | M | T | W | T | F | S |
|---|---|---|---|---|---|---|
| | | | | | | 1 |
| 2 | 3 | 4 | 5 | 6 | 7 | 8 |
| 9 | 10 | 11 | 12 | 13 | 14 | 15 |
| 16 | 17 | 18 | 19 | 20 | 21 | 22 |
| 23 | 24 | 25 | 26 | 27 | 28 | 29 |
| 30 | 31 | | | | | |

### 2022

All things work together for those that love God. -Romans 8:28

Sunday 2

Monday 3

Tuesday 4

Wednesday 5

# October 2022

## Thursday 6

## Friday 7

## Saturday 8

### October

| S | M | T | W | T | F | S |
|---|---|---|---|---|---|---|
|   |   |   |   |   |   | 1 |
| 2 | 3 | 4 | 5 | 6 | 7 | 8 |
| 9 | 10 | 11 | 12 | 13 | 14 | 15 |
| 16 | 17 | 18 | 19 | 20 | 21 | 22 |
| 23 | 24 | 25 | 26 | 27 | 28 | 29 |
| 30 | 31 |   |   |   |   |   |

### 2022

All things work together for those that love God. -Romans 8:28

| Sunday | 9 |
| Monday | 10 |

Columbus Day

| Tuesday | 11 |
| Wednesday | 12 |

## Thursday 13

## Friday 14

## Saturday 15

### October

| S | M | T | W | T | F | S |
|---|---|---|---|---|---|---|
| | | | | | | 1 |
| 2 | 3 | 4 | 5 | 6 | 7 | 8 |
| 9 | 10 | 11 | 12 | 13 | 14 | 15 |
| 16 | 17 | 18 | 19 | 20 | 21 | 22 |
| 23 | 24 | 25 | 26 | 27 | 28 | 29 |
| 30 | 31 | | | | | |

### 2022

Sunday 16

Monday 17

Tuesday 18

Wednesday 19

## Thursday 20

## Friday 21

## Saturday 22

## October

| S | M | T | W | T | F | S |
|---|---|---|---|---|---|---|
|   |   |   |   |   |   | 1 |
| 2 | 3 | 4 | 5 | 6 | 7 | 8 |
| 9 | 10 | 11 | 12 | 13 | 14 | 15 |
| 16 | 17 | 18 | 19 | 20 | 21 | 22 |
| 23 | 24 | 25 | 26 | 27 | 28 | 29 |
| 30 | 31 |   |   |   |   |   |

### 2022

All things work together for those that love God. -Romans 8:28

| | |
|---|---|
| Sunday *23* | Monday *24* |
| Tuesday *25* | Wednesday *26* |

## Thursday 27

## Friday 28

## Saturday 29

### October

| S | M | T | W | T | F | S |
|---|---|---|---|---|---|---|
| | | | | | | 1 |
| 2 | 3 | 4 | 5 | 6 | 7 | 8 |
| 9 | 10 | 11 | 12 | 13 | 14 | 15 |
| 16 | 17 | 18 | 19 | 20 | 21 | 22 |
| 23 | 24 | 25 | 26 | 27 | 28 | 29 |
| 30 | 31 | | | | | |

### 2022

## Cucumber Water
~Keeps away bad breath
~Aids in weight loss
~Protects the body from cancer
~Great source of antioxidants

### INGREDIENTS:
water
2 cucumbers
1 lemon
mint leaves

### INSTRUCTIONS:
~Cut the cucumbers into slices
~Cut up lemon into slices
~In pitcher, add cucumber and
lemon slices
~Pour water into pitcher
~Garnish top with a few fresh
mint leaves
~Enjoy!

# WHERE FOCUS GOES
## energy flows

**goal:**

**STEP 1:**

**STEP 2:**

**STEP 3:**

A *goal* WITHOUT A *plan* IS A *wish*

# Gratitude List

♡

♡

♡

♡

♡

## STAY PATIENT
and trust your journey

# Stuff I Need to Remember

_____

_____

_____

_____

_____

_____

_____

_____

_____

_____

The will of God will never take you where
the grace of God will not protect you.

| Sunday | Monday | Tuesday | Wednesday |
|--------|--------|---------|-----------|
|        |        | 1       | 2         |
| 6      | 7      | 8       | 9         |
| Daylight Savings Ends | | | |
| 13     | 14     | 15      | 16        |
| 20     | 21     | 22      | 23        |
| 27     | 28     | 29      | 30        |

| Thursday | Friday | Saturday |
|---|---|---|
| 3 | 4 | 5 |
| 10 | 11<br><br>Veterans Day | 12 |
| 17 | 18 | 19 |
| 24<br><br>Thanksgiving | 25 | 26 |
|  |  |  |

November
2022

Sunday                                    30

Monday                                    31

Halloween

Tuesday                                    1

Wednesday                                 2

Thursday 3

Friday 4

Saturday 5

## November

| S | M | T | W | T | F | S |
|---|---|---|---|---|---|---|
|   |   | 1 | 2 | 3 | 4 | 5 |
| 6 | 7 | 8 | 9 | 10 | 11 | 12 |
| 13 | 14 | 15 | 16 | 17 | 18 | 19 |
| 20 | 21 | 22 | 23 | 24 | 25 | 26 |
| 27 | 28 | 29 | 30 |   |   |   |

### 2022

Sunday 6

Daylight Savings Ends

Monday 7

Tuesday 8

Wednesday 9

# November 2022

## Thursday 10

## Friday 11

Veterans Day

## Saturday 12

## November

| S | M | T | W | T | F | S |
|---|---|---|---|---|---|---|
|  |  | 1 | 2 | 3 | 4 | 5 |
| 6 | 7 | 8 | 9 | 10 | 11 | 12 |
| 13 | 14 | 15 | 16 | 17 | 18 | 19 |
| 20 | 21 | 22 | 23 | 24 | 25 | 26 |
| 27 | 28 | 29 | 30 |  |  |  |

## 2022

Tell God what you need, thank him for all he has done. -Phillipians 4:

## Sunday 13

## Monday 14

## Tuesday 15

## Wednesday 16

Thursday 17

Friday 18

Saturday 19

## November

| S | M | T | W | T | F | S |
|---|---|---|---|---|---|---|
|   |   | 1 | 2 | 3 | 4 | 5 |
| 6 | 7 | 8 | 9 | 10 | 11 | 12 |
| 13 | 14 | 15 | 16 | 17 | 18 | 19 |
| 20 | 21 | 22 | 23 | 24 | 25 | 26 |
| 27 | 28 | 29 | 30 |   |   |   |

### 2o22

Sunday 20

Monday 21

Tuesday 22

Wednesday 23

## Thursday 24

Thanksgiving

## Friday 25

## Saturday 26

### November

| S | M | T | W | T | F | S |
|---|---|---|---|---|---|---|
|   |   | 1 | 2 | 3 | 4 | 5 |
| 6 | 7 | 8 | 9 | 10 | 11 | 12 |
| 13 | 14 | 15 | 16 | 17 | 18 | 19 |
| 20 | 21 | 22 | 23 | 24 | 25 | 26 |
| 27 | 28 | 29 | 30 |   |   |   |

### 2022

# WHERE FOCUS GOES
*energy flows*

**goal:**

**STEP 1:**

**STEP 2:**

**STEP 3:**

A *goal* WITHOUT A *plan* IS A *wish*

# Gratitude List

♡

♡

♡

♡

♡

## EACH DAY
*is a new beginning*

# Stuff I Need to Remember

_____

_____

_____

_____

_____

_____

_____

_____

_____

_____

Get into the habit of asking yourself, "does this support the life I'm trying to create?"

| Sunday | Monday | Tuesday | Wednesday |
|--------|--------|---------|-----------|
|  |  |  |  |
| 4 | 5 | 6 | 7 |
| 11 | 12 | 13 | 14 |
| 18 | 19 | 20 | 21 |
| 25<br>Christmas Day | 26<br>Kwanzaa Begins | 27 | 28 |

| Thursday | Friday | Saturday |
|---|---|---|
| 1 | 2 | 3 |
| 8 | 9 | 10 |
| 15 | 16 | 17 |
| 22 | 23 | 24<br><br>Christmas Eve |
| 29 | 30 | 31<br><br>New Year's Eve |

December

2022

Sunday 27

Monday 28

Tuesday 29

Wednesday 30

Thursday 1

Friday 2

Saturday 3

## December

| S | M | T | W | T | F | S |
|---|---|---|---|---|---|---|
|   |   |   |   | 1 | 2 | 3 |
| 4 | 5 | 6 | 7 | 8 | 9 | 10 |
| 11 | 12 | 13 | 14 | 15 | 16 | 17 |
| 18 | 19 | 20 | 21 | 22 | 23 | 24 |
| 25 | 26 | 27 | 28 | 29 | 30 | 31 |

### 2022

Sunday

4

Monday

5

Tuesday

6

Wednesday

7

## Thursday 8

## Friday 9

## Saturday 10

## December

| S | M | T | W | T | F | S |
|---|---|---|---|---|---|---|
| | | | | 1 | 2 | 3 |
| 4 | 5 | 6 | 7 | 8 | 9 | 10 |
| 11 | 12 | 13 | 14 | 15 | 16 | 17 |
| 18 | 19 | 20 | 21 | 22 | 23 | 24 |
| 25 | 26 | 27 | 28 | 29 | 30 | 31 |

### 2022

## Sunday 11

## Monday 12

## Tuesday 13

## Wednesday 14

## Thursday 15

## Friday 16

## Saturday 17

### December

| S | M | T | W | T | F | S |
|---|---|---|---|---|---|---|
| | | | | 1 | 2 | 3 |
| 4 | 5 | 6 | 7 | 8 | 9 | 10 |
| 11 | 12 | 13 | 14 | 15 | 16 | 17 |
| 18 | 19 | 20 | 21 | 22 | 23 | 24 |
| 25 | 26 | 27 | 28 | 29 | 30 | 31 |

## 2022

## Sunday 18

## Monday 19

## Tuesday 20

## Wednesday 21

## Thursday 22

## Friday 23

## Saturday 24

Christmas Eve

## December

| S | M | T | W | T | F | S |
|---|---|---|---|---|---|---|
| | | | | 1 | 2 | 3 |
| 4 | 5 | 6 | 7 | 8 | 9 | 10 |
| 11 | 12 | 13 | 14 | 15 | 16 | 17 |
| 18 | 19 | 20 | 21 | 22 | 23 | 24 |
| 25 | 26 | 27 | 28 | 29 | 30 | 31 |

### 2022

# Nothing is impossible with God. -Luke 1:37

## Sunday 25

Christmas

## Monday 26

Kwanzaa Begins

## Tuesday 27

## Wednesday 28

Thursday **29**

Friday **30**

Saturday **31**

New Year's Eve

## December

| S | M | T | W | T | F | S |
|---|---|---|---|---|---|---|
|   |   |   |   | 1 | 2 | 3 |
| 4 | 5 | 6 | 7 | 8 | 9 | 10 |
| 11 | 12 | 13 | 14 | 15 | 16 | 17 |
| 18 | 19 | 20 | 21 | 22 | 23 | 24 |
| 25 | 26 | 27 | 28 | 29 | 30 | 31 |

### 2022

# IMPORTANT CONTACTS

Name
Number
Email
Birthday

Name
Number
Email
Birthday

Name
Number
Email
Birthday

Name
Number
Email
Birthday

Name
Number
Email
Birthday

Name
Number
Email
Birthday

Name
Number
Email
Birthday

Company:

Account #

Username:

Password/Pin:


Company:

Account #

Username:

Password/Pin:


Company:

Account #

Username:

Password/Pin:


Company:

Account #

Username:

Password/Pin:


Company:

Account #

Username:

Password/Pin:


Company:

Account #

Username:

Password/Pin:

UTILITIES & SERVICES

# IMPORTANT PASSWORDS

**WiFi**

**a**

**P**

**$**

**hulu**

IMPORTANT PASSWORDS

# Meet the Artist

**W**ith an artistic individuality all her own, artist Sylvia "Gbaby" Phillips, founder of Gbaby™, purposes her art as an apparatus built to inspire, encourage, and spark motivation in all that encounter each one-of-a-kind piece. Sylvia continues to stay true to her signature by creating visual eloquence in every bold and powerful image of a woman she paints. With its exclusive hand-painted handbags conquered, the Gbaby brand has launched into a new medium to expand the collection still with hopes to edify all who see.

• • • • •

**S**ylvia has celebrated a career that has taken her around the country to various festivals, including the Essence, National Black Arts, Chicago Music and Art, and Pan African Film Festivals. She has also created a logo for BET's Black Girls Rock. The message and beauty of her paintings resonates with men and women around the country.

• • • • •

**N**ow living in Conyers, Georgia, Sylvia plans to continue to spread the Gbaby™ influence around the south. She is continuing on with her original paintings and mixed media masks. With three licensing deals, her artwork is produced on an array of products including: cutting boards, light switch covers, mugs & bottles, inspirational cards, journals, stationery, home decor, calendars, inspirational planners, bags, and accessories, so that everyone can "Feel the heART."